Meet Farm Animals

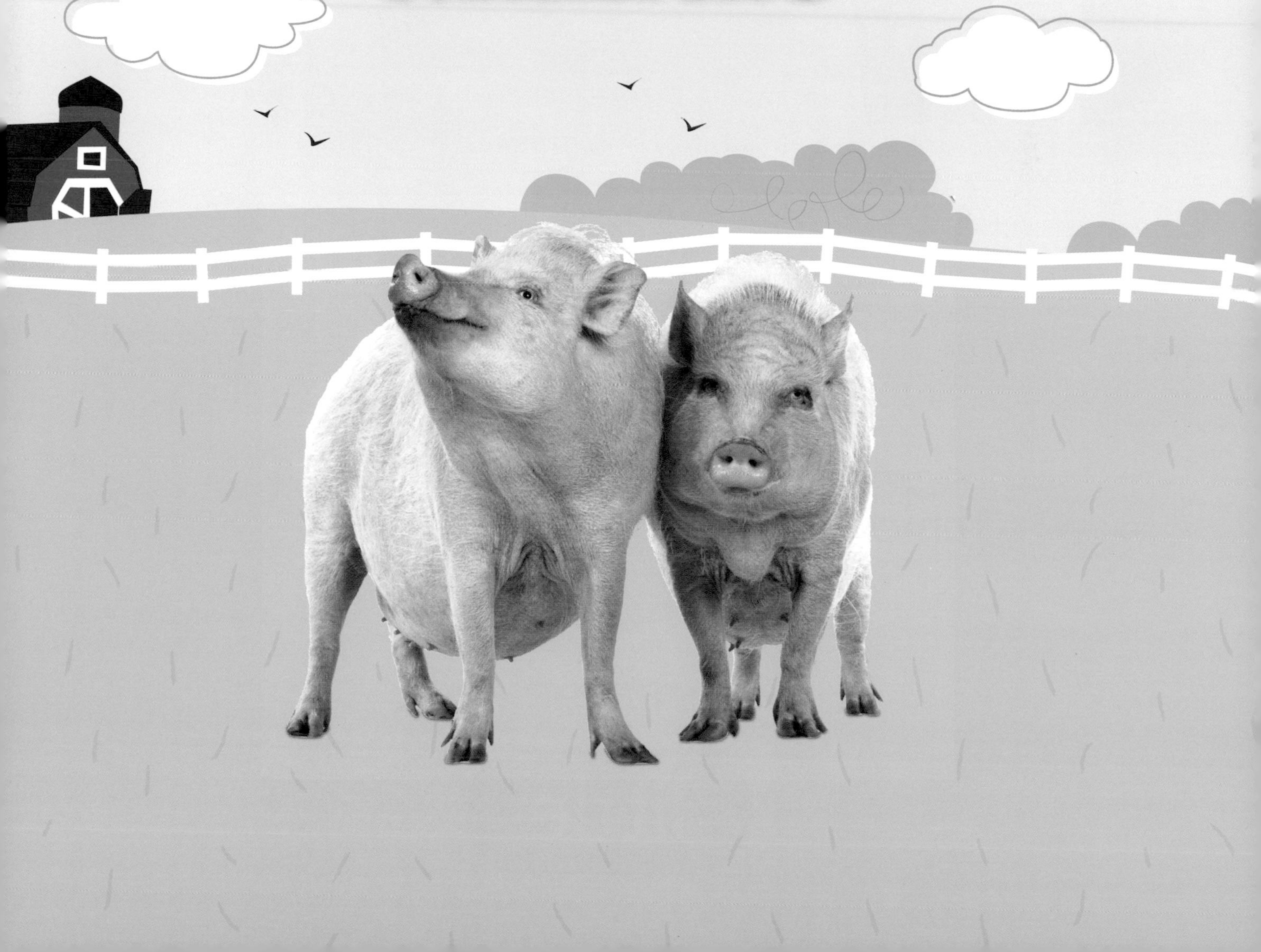

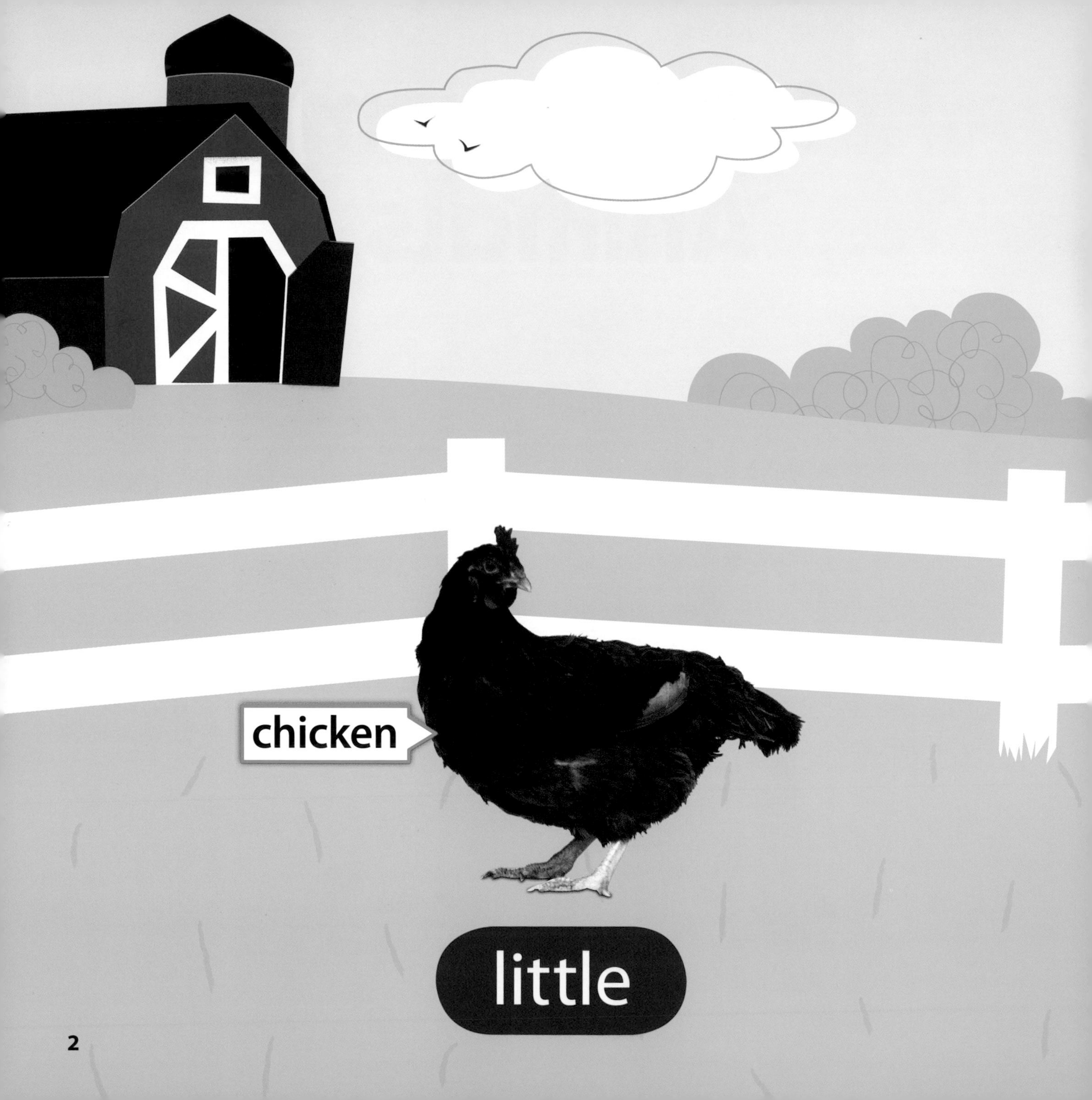

little

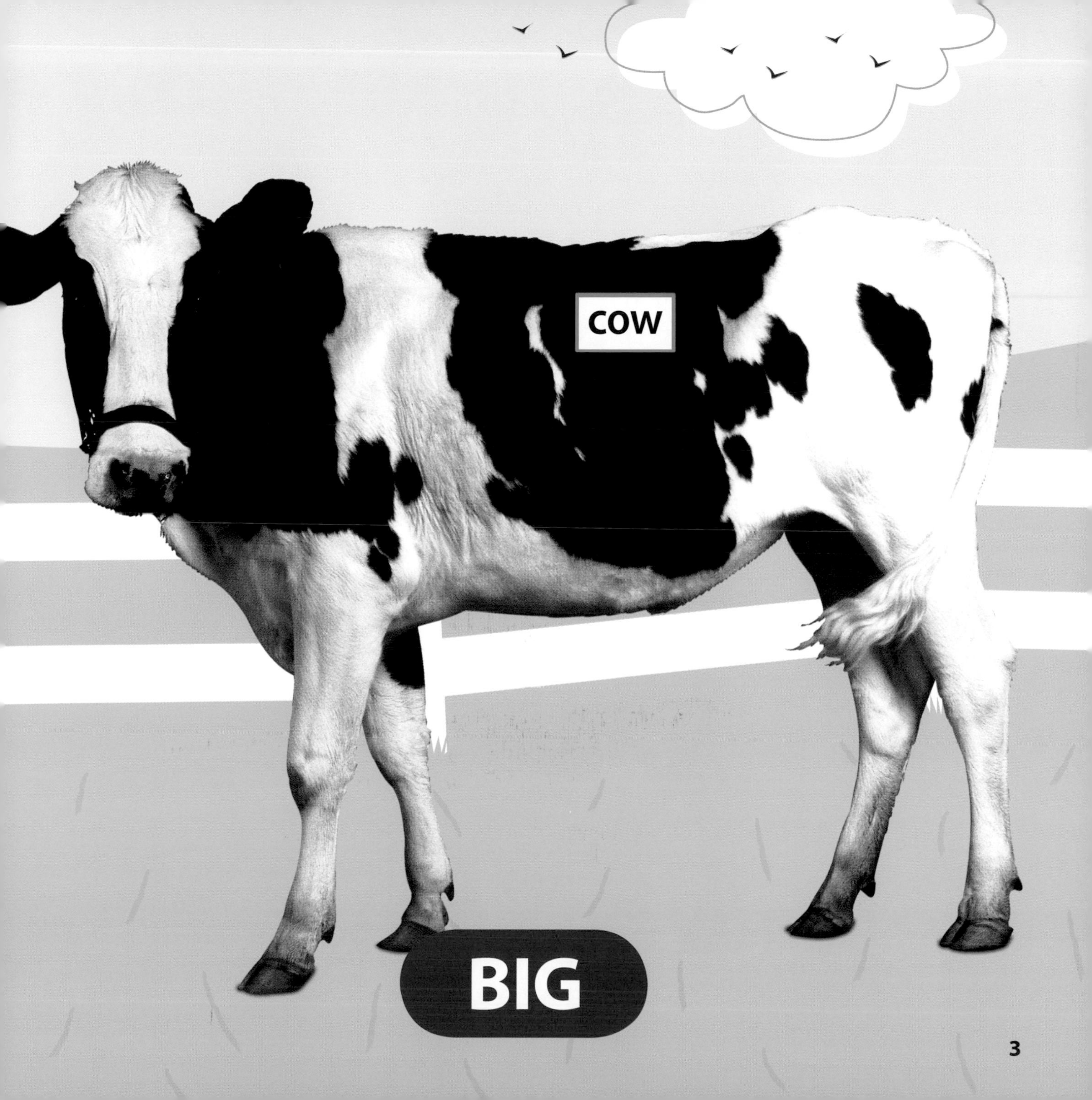

BIG

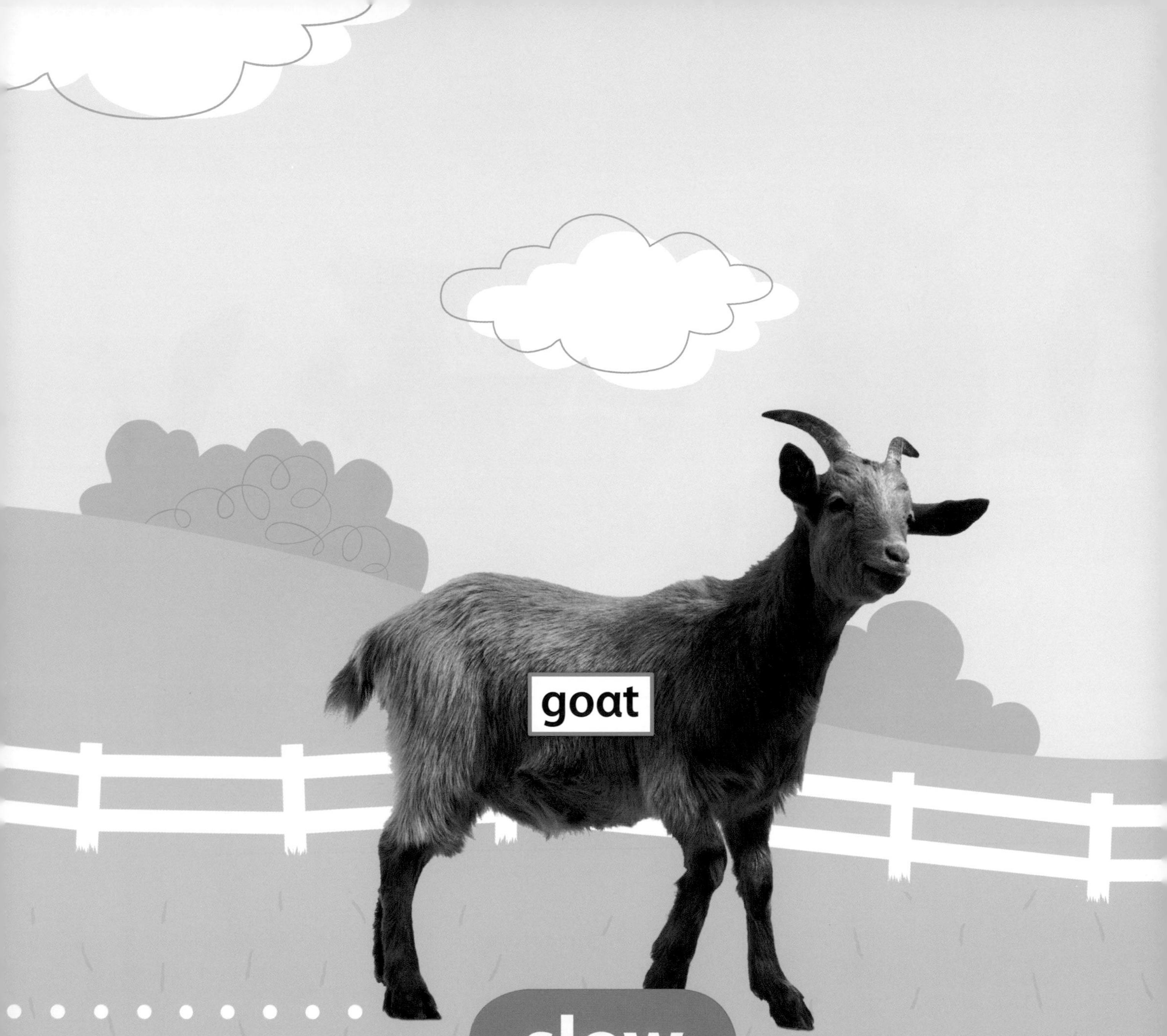

slow

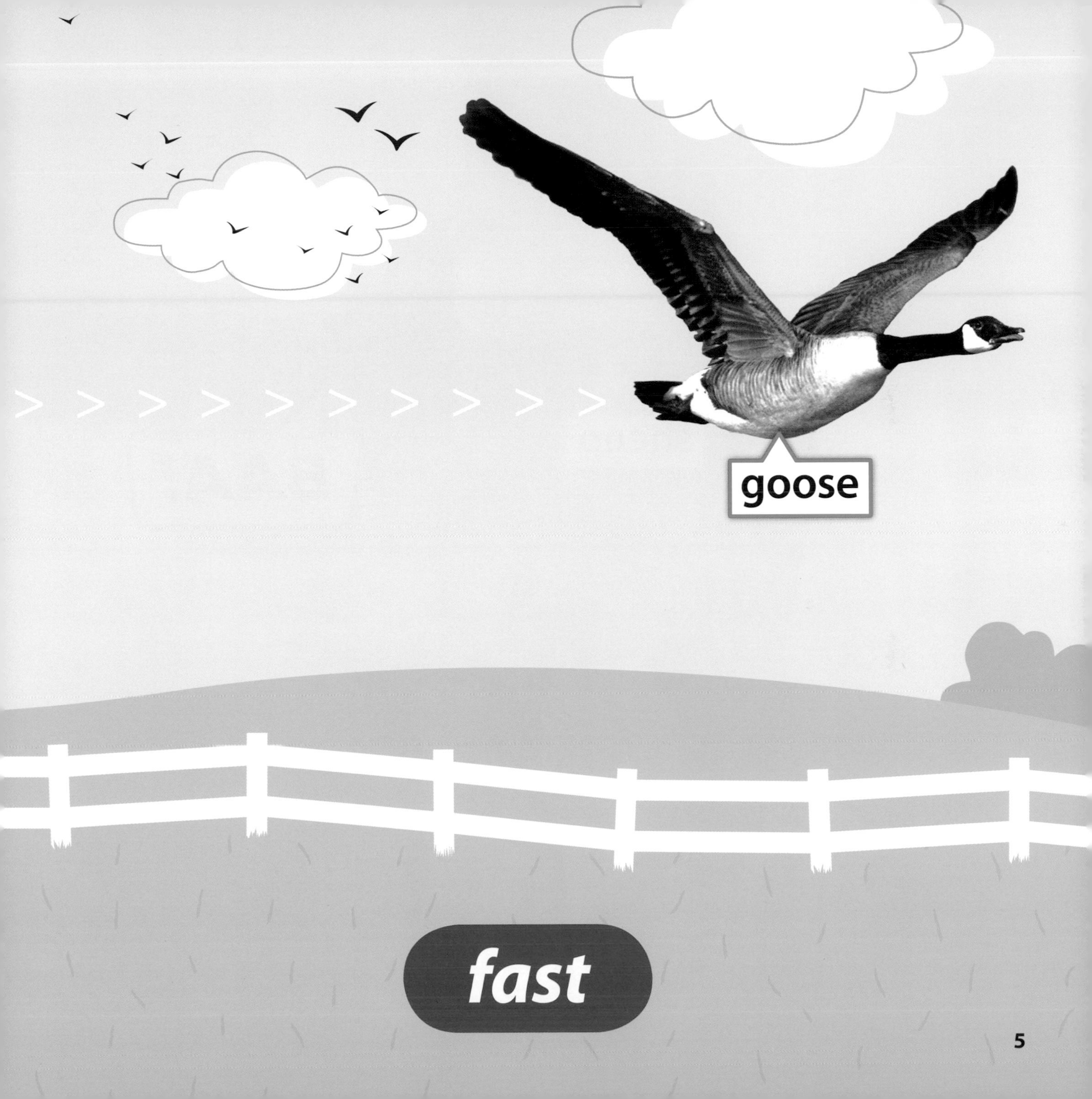

fast

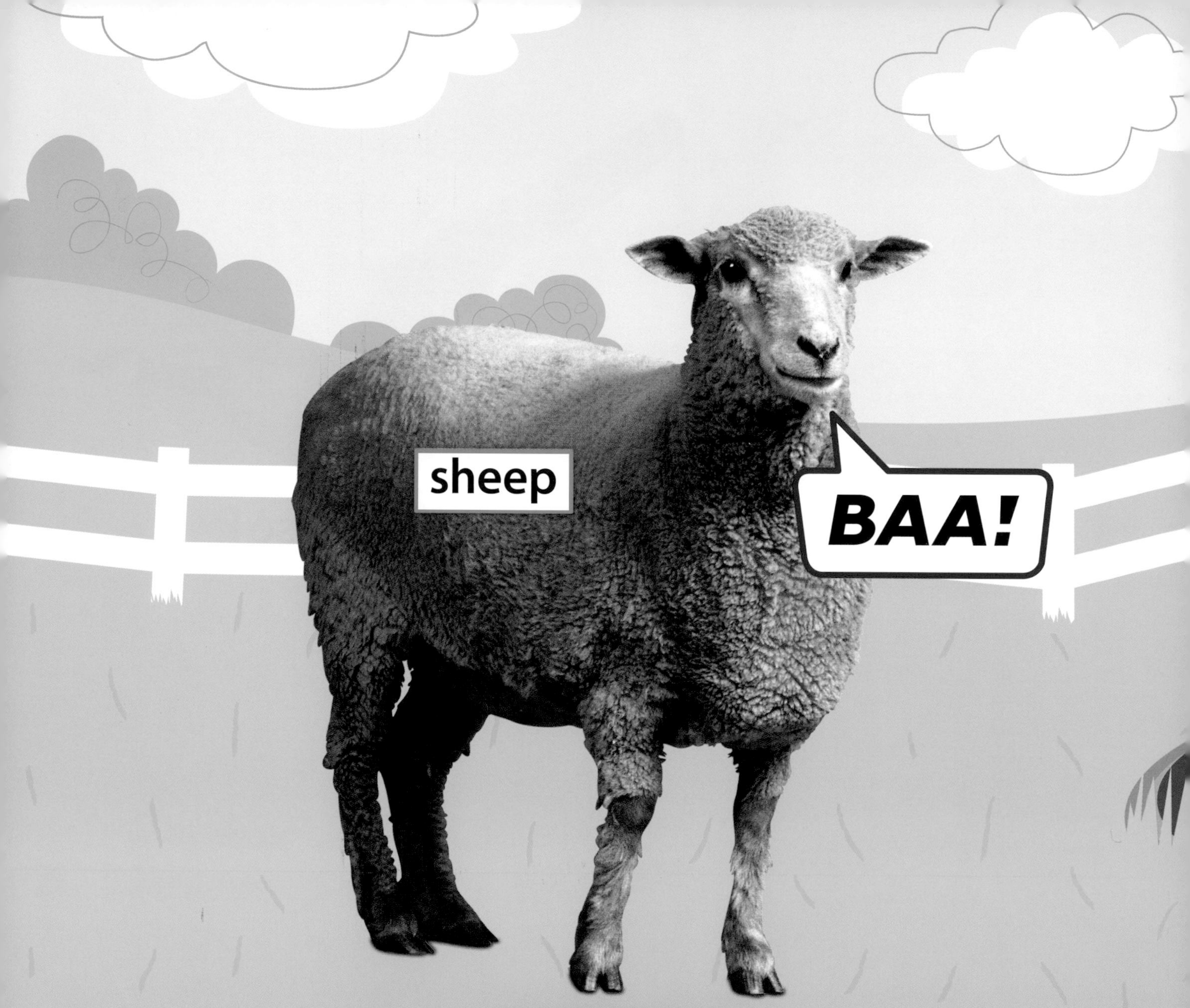

LOUD

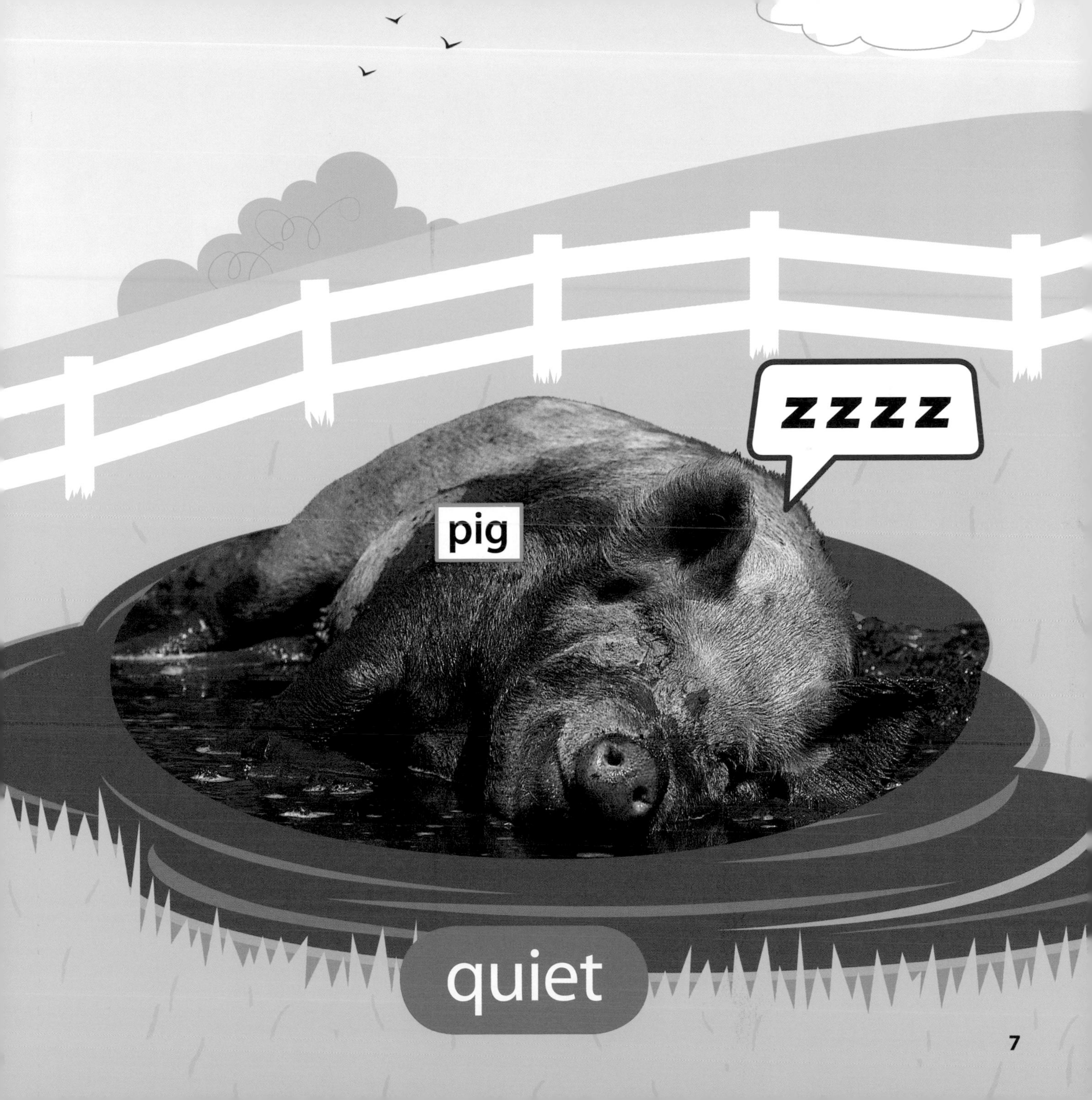

quiet

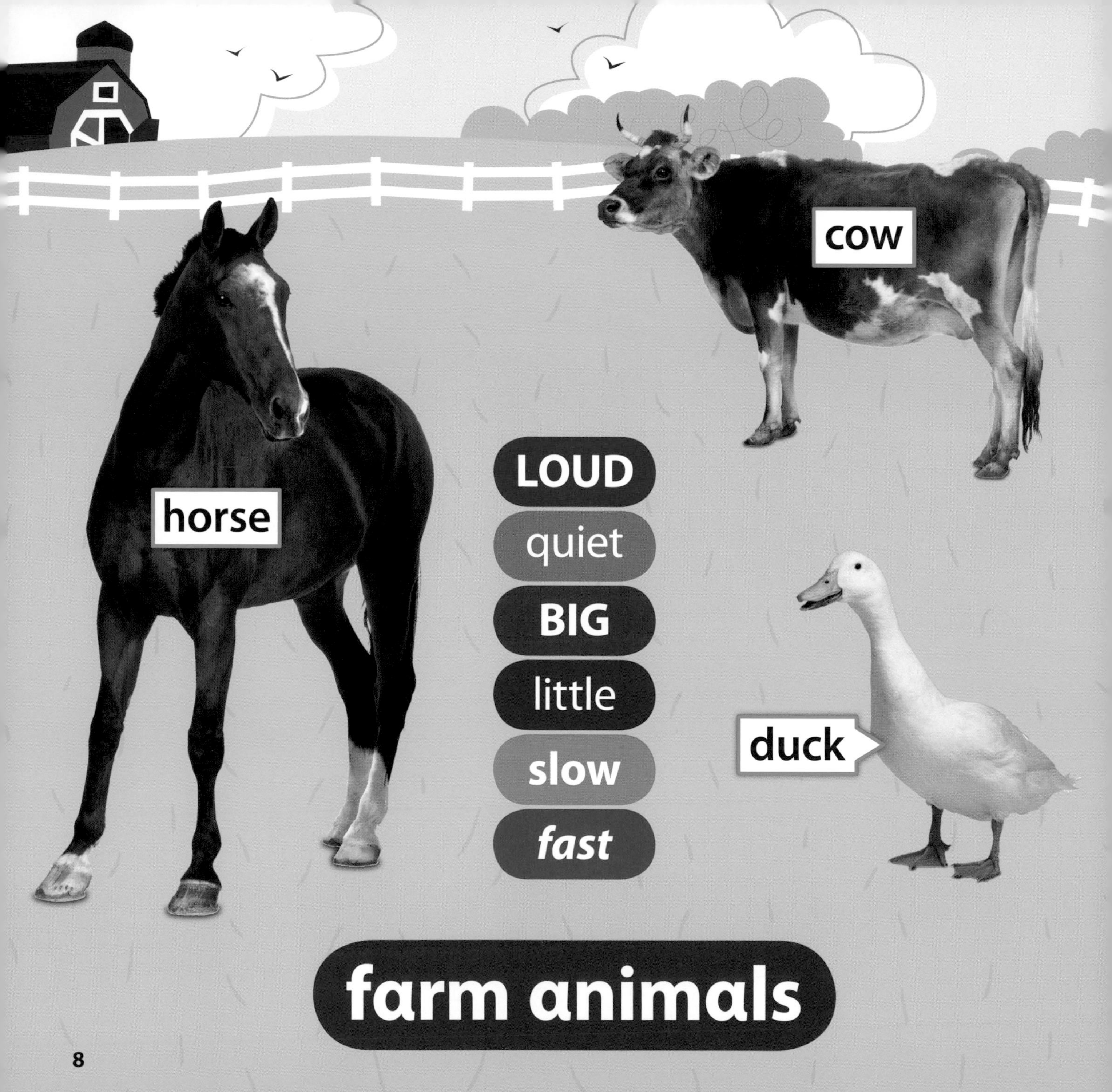

LOUD

quiet

BIG

little

slow

fast

farm animals